LET'S INVESTIGATE
Time, Distance and Speed

LET'S INVESTIGATE
Time, Distance and Speed

By Marion Smoothey

Illustrated by Ted Evans

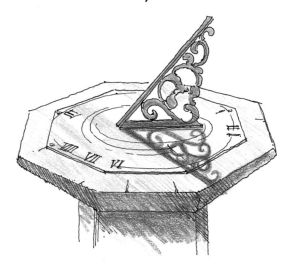

MARSHALL CAVENDISH
NEW YORK · LONDON · TORONTO · SYDNEY

Library Edition Published 1993

© Marshall Cavendish Corporation 1993

Published by Marshall Cavendish Corporation
2415 Jerusalem Avenue
PO Box 587
North Bellmore
New York 11710

Series created by Graham Beehag Book Design

Library of Congress Cataloging-in-Publication Data

Smoothey, Marion, 1943-
    Time, distance, and speed / by Marion Smoothey; illustrated by Ted Evans.
        p. cm.. -- (Let's Investigate)
    Includes index.
    Summary: Text and activities explain how time, distance, and speed can be measured .
    ISBN 1-85435-467-1 ISBN 1-85435-463-9 (set)
    1. Time -- Measurement -- Miscellanea -- Juvenile literature.
    2. Distances -- Measurement -- Miscellanea -- Juvenile literature.
    3. Speed -- Measurement -- Miscellanea -- Juvenile literature.
    [1. Time -- Measurement. 2. Distances -- Measurement.
    3. Speed -- Measurement.]
    I. Evans, Ted ill. II. Title. III. Series:
Smoothey, Marion, 1943- Let's Investigate.
Q163.S59 1993   92-36225
529' . 7---dc20   CIP
                                                 AC

Printed in Malaysia by Times Offset (M) SDN BHD
Bound in the United States

Contents

Not all problems are what they seem!

A frog is at the bottom of a 40 foot well. Each hour he climbs up 5 feet and then slips back 4 feet. How many hours does it take him to get out?

A band of thirty musicians takes five minutes to play a dance. How long will a band of forty-five musicians take?

Marking Time

8

We mark off our lives in lengths of time. These are related to the movement of the Earth around the Sun, and of the Moon around the Earth.

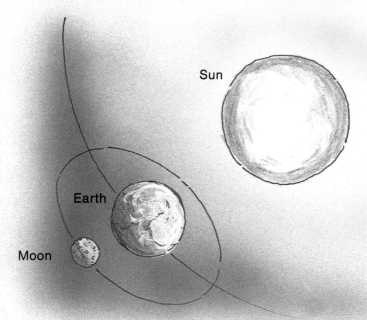

Days

A day is the length of time the Earth takes to spin around its own axis. Its axis is an imaginary line passing through it from the North to the South poles. When our side of the Earth is facing the Sun, we have daylight. Night time is when our side of the Earth is facing away from the Sun.

The Earth travels around the Sun. The Moon travels around the Earth. At the same time the Moon and Earth are spinning on their own axes.

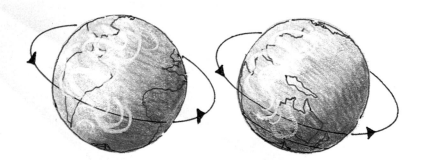

Hours

The Egyptians, in about 4000 B.C., were probably the first to divide a day into twenty-four hours. Their hours were not all the same length. The lengths of the hours varied according to the time of year because they depended on the movement of the Sun.

Since then people have divided the day into twenty-four equal hours beginning at midnight. Each hour is divided into sixty minutes. There are sixty seconds in a minute.

Years

A year is the length of time it takes the Earth to travel once around the Sun. The Earth travels 580 million miles at an average speed of 66,000 miles per hour in its **orbit** around the Sun.

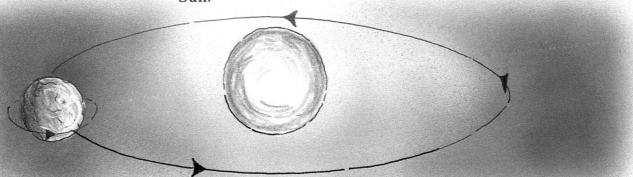

It takes the Earth approximately one year to make the journey around the Sun. At the same time the Earth is spinning around its own axis once each day.

A problem arises because there is not a whole number of days that exactly fills a year. A year has approximately 365 days, 5 hours, 48 minutes and 45.4 seconds, or nearly $365\frac{1}{4}$ days. To make marking time simpler we have leap years.

Leap years

A year consists of 365 days for three years in a row. In the fourth year we add on an extra day to make up for the parts of days not counted during the past three years. This extra day is February 29.

This still does not quite balance out, so the year at the end of each **century** is not counted as a leap year unless it can be divided exactly by 400. The year 1900 was not a leap year; 2000 will be a leap year.

You can always work out whether or not a particular year is a leap year by dividing the last two digits by 4. If there is no remainder, the year is a leap year, unless it follows the end of a century.

Was 1531 a leap year?

$31 \div 4 = 7 \text{ r } 3$.

There is a remainder, so 1531 was not a leap year.

● When was the next leap year after 1531?

● **1.** Will 2150 be a leap year?

● **2.** Why do you need to look only at the last two numbers to decide whether or not a year is a leap year?

● **3.** Selina has just had her third birthday. How old is she?

10

● **4.** Was 1200 a leap year?

Months

A month is the time the Moon takes to travel once around the Earth. If you watch the Moon all through a month you will see that it appears to change shape. These changes are called the phases of the Moon.

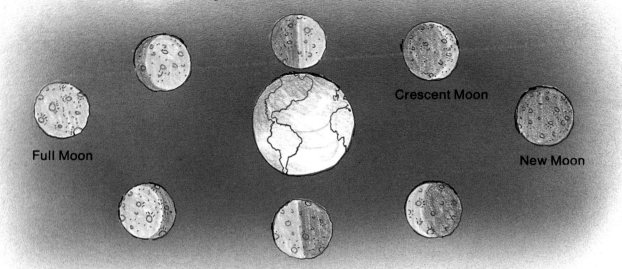

Full Moon

Crescent Moon

New Moon

As the Moon makes its monthly journey around the Earth, its appearance to us on Earth changes from a circle to a thin crescent. This is because the amount of light from the Sun falling on the Moon varies as the relating position of the Earth, Moon and Sun change.

◇ If you are outside at night, you can imitate the shapes of the Moon by using a white ball and a flashlight. Rest the flashlight where it will stay pointing at you. Have a friend walk around you while holding the white ball up in the light. You will see that the shape on the ball which is lit up changes from a thin crescent to a circle.

The length of time between each new Moon is approximately 29 days and is called a **lunar month**.

● How many days are there in twelve lunar months?

To solve the problem that twelve lunar months do not exactly make a year, we have the twelve **calendar months**.

This rhyme can help you to remember how many days there are in each calendar month.

> *Thirty days hath September,*
> *April, June and November.*
> *All the rest have thirty-one,*
> *Except February alone.*
> *That has twenty-eight days clear*
> *And twenty-nine in a leap year.*

Timers

12

One of the earliest devices to measure time was the sundial. While the Sun appears to move across the sky during the course of a day (what is really happening?), the length of the shadow made by a stick changes.

By measuring these changes in length, people were able to make sundials.

The large **obelisks** found in the cities of the ancient Egyptians were put up for this purpose. The shadows that they cast were used to tell the time. Cleopatra's Needle, which was taken from Egypt and placed in London, is one of these.

● **1.** Look at the shadows cast by trees or tall apartment buildings at different times of day. When are the shadows shortest?

● **2.** Sundials have one obvious disadvantage. What is it?

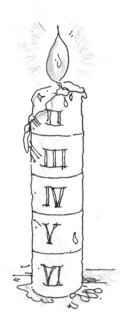

Wax, sand and water were also used to make timers. Look at how these work.

◇ You can make each of these for yourself.

A calibrated candle

Ask an adult to watch you do this.

You need:
a candle which is straight, not tapered, a ruler, a pin, a piece of modeling clay, and a shallow dish.

With the ruler, measure the length of the candle. Put the clay on the bottom of the candle. Place the candle securely in the dish, out of drafts. Light it.

Allow the candle to burn for half an hour. Blow out the candle. Allow it to cool and the melted wax to harden again. Measure the candle again and figure out how much it has burned away during the half hour. This is the length the candle should burn down every half hour.

With the pin, mark on the candle where it will burn down to every half hour.

You can use your calibrated candle to make as many more similar ones as you like.

● **1.** Why must they all be the same shape and size?

● **2.** Why must you keep the candle out of drafts?

14

A water clock

The water clock was one of the earliest answers to the problem of making a timer that worked when the sun was not shining. This was invented in about 1500 B.C. You can make one out of a clean empty can, a clean empty jar, a hammer and a nail and a pencil.

◇ Stick a piece of paper on the jar so that you can mark a scale on it. Make a small hole in the bottom of the can with the point of the nail. Fill the can with water. Balance it carefully on the jar.

◇ Every quarter of an hour mark the height of the water in the jar.

A sand timer

Sand timers were invented soon after water clocks. To make one you need some dry sand or salt, some adhesive tape and a piece of paper.

◇ Make the paper into a cone with a small hole in the bottom. Fasten the cone with the adhesive tape.

◇ Fill the cone with sand or salt. Mark the level it reaches. Allow the sand to trickle out into a container. When each minute goes by, mark the level of the remaining sand on the cone.

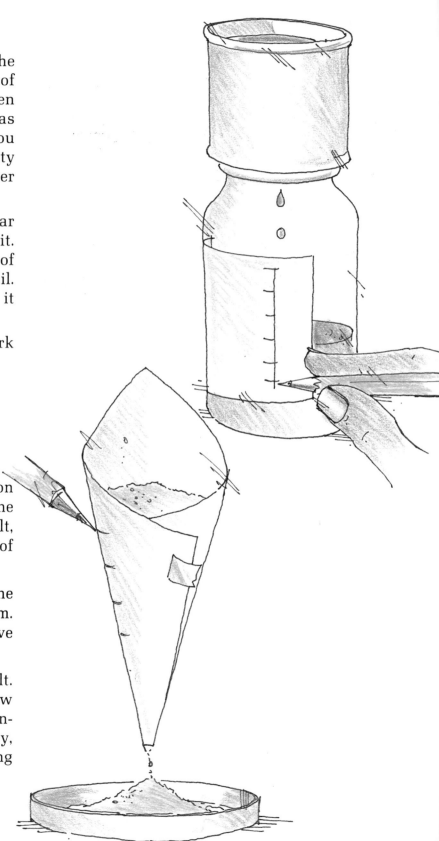

Your own timer

◇ Can you design a timer of your own?

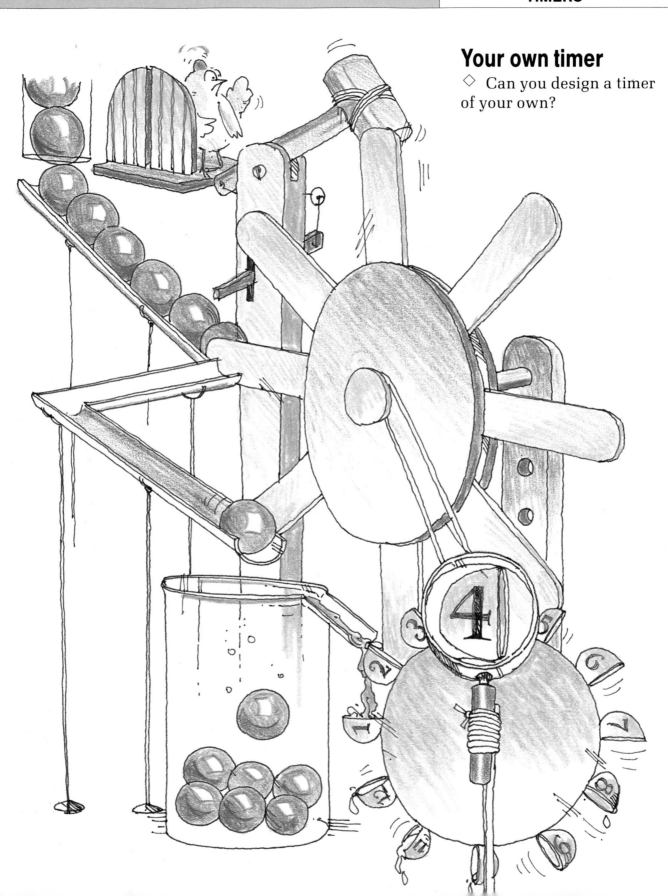

Telling the Time

Telling the time can be confusing. There are different shaped clocks and watches, different numbers and marks on the faces and different ways of saying the time. The picture shows different ways of telling the time. See if you can match them together with the list below.

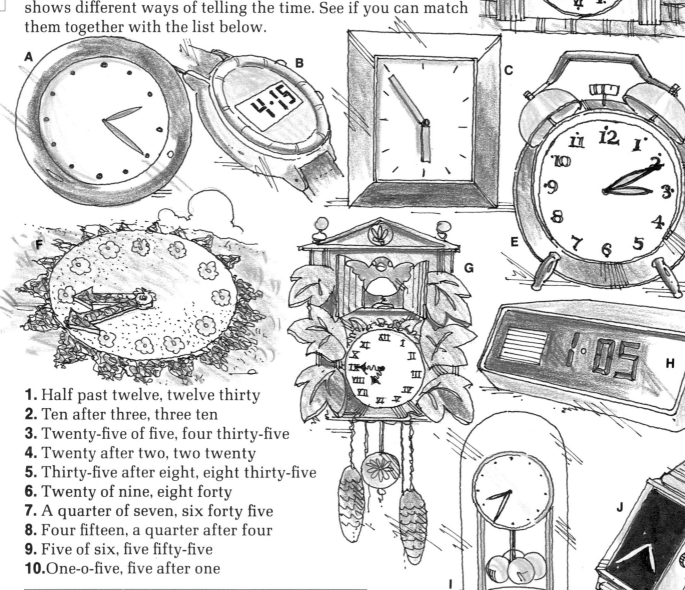

1. Half past twelve, twelve thirty
2. Ten after three, three ten
3. Twenty-five of five, four thirty-five
4. Twenty after two, two twenty
5. Thirty-five after eight, eight thirty-five
6. Twenty of nine, eight forty
7. A quarter of seven, six forty five
8. Four fifteen, a quarter after four
9. Five of six, five fifty-five
10. One-o-five, five after one

Check your answers on page 18.

Dinner Time

Hamburgers are on the menu today. The grill holds two at a time. Each hamburger takes five minutes to cook on each side.

● **1.** How long does it take to cook two hamburgers?

● **2.** How long does the quickest way of cooking three hamburgers under the grill take?

● **3.** Dad needs to cook seven hamburgers and have them ready at half past six. At what time does he need to start cooking?

Turn to page 20.

Answers to page 16

These are the clocks and times that match.
A and **4**
B and **8**
C and **9**
D and **1**
E and **2**
F and **6**
G and **7**
H and **10**
I and **5**
J and **3**

> **If you got most of them correct, you can go back to page 17.**
> **If you made five or more mistakes, read these reminders and try the puzzle opposite.**

The long hand tells you the number of minutes.

The short hand tells you the number of hours.

The hour hand moves slowly, only part of the way from one number to the next, as the minute hand goes around the clock once. At half past any hour, the hour hand is halfway between two numbers.

Justin Time

Each clock has several routes leading away from it.

- Choose the route that has the correct time on it and move to the next clock.
- Which of the boys is Justin Time?

19

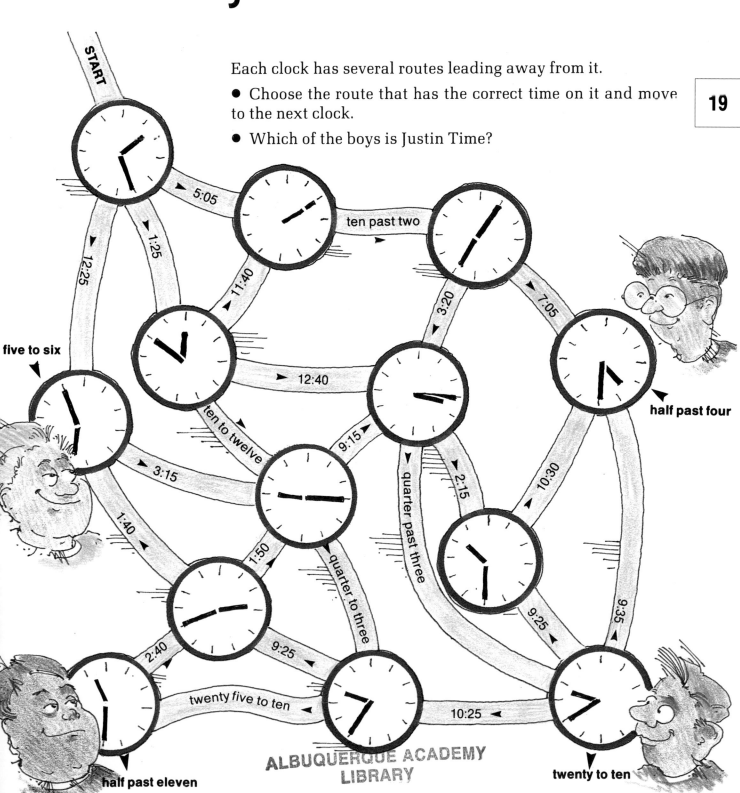

Bussed or Bust?

Ann and Wayne need to catch the eight o'clock bus to work in the morning.

Ann thinks her watch is 10 minutes slow. It is actually 10 minutes fast. Wayne's watch is 10 minutes slow. He thinks it is 10 minutes fast.

● They each leave home at what they think is the correct time to catch the bus. Who will miss it?

Odd Pairs Out

In this row of clocks, **B** and **C** are the odd pair out because there is a thirty minute interval between the times shown on each of the other clocks.

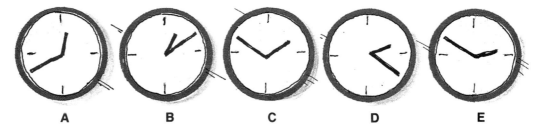

    A   B   C   D   E

● In each set of five clocks, there is an odd pair. Which are they?

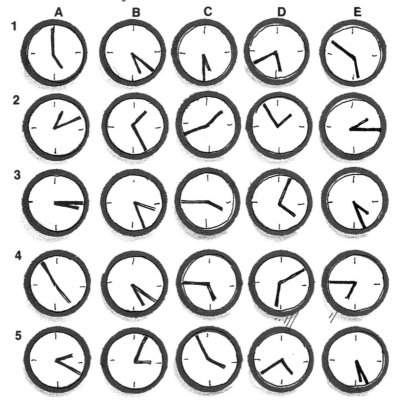

22

Answers to page 21

The odd pairs out are:
1. A & B 20 minutes instead of 10
2. D & E 20 minutes instead of 15
3. A & B 10 minutes instead of 20
4. D & E 35 minutes instead of 25
5. B & C 50 minutes instead of 45

Answers to Dinner Time

1. It takes 10 minutes to cook two hamburgers. You put them both on the grill together and cook them for 5 minutes each side.

2. The quickest way of cooking three hamburgers takes 15 minutes. You put two on the grill and cook one side for 5 minutes. You remove one partly-cooked hamburger, turn over the other one and put on the uncooked hamburger. Grill them for 5 minutes. Remove the cooked hamburger, return the half-cooked hamburger which you removed. Place both hamburgers, uncooked side up, under the grill for a further 5 minutes.

3. Dad can cook four hamburgers by method 1 which takes 20 minutes. He can cook the remaining three by method 2 which takes 15 minutes. He needs to start 35 minutes before six thirty, which is five of six.

Answers to Bussed or Bust

Wayne is the one who missed the bus.

Assume they each need 15 minutes to get to the bus stop.

Ann needs to leave at 7:45 a.m. She thinks she needs to leave when her watch says 7:35. When her watch says 7:35, the time is really 7:25. She leaves at 7:25 and arrives at the bus stop at 7:40 p.m. She has 20 minutes to wait for the bus.

Wayne thinks he needs to leave when his watch says 7:55. This is really 8:05 a.m. He will be 20 minutes late.

It doesn't matter how long they need to get to the bus stop. If they leave at the correct time, Ann will be twenty minutes early and Wayne will be twenty minutes late.

Twenty-four Hour Clock

24

In everyday use we generally split the day up into two periods of twelve hours to tell the time. After 12:59 we start again at 1:00.

In order to distinguish between 10 o'clock in the morning and 10 o'clock at night, we use a.m. and p.m.: "a.m." is short for "*ante meridiem*," which is Latin for "before noon;" "a.m. can also stand for "after midnight;" "p.m." stands for "*post meridiem*," which means "after noon."

Ten o'clock in the morning is 10:00 a.m. Ten o'clock at night is 10:00 p.m. Twelve noon is 12:00 p.m. Twelve o'clock midnight is 12:00 a.m.

Many digital watches and timetables use the twenty-four hour clock. In this system, the times of the day use all twenty-four hours. The next minute after 12:59 in the afternoon is 13:00. In the twenty-four hour clock, you always use four numbers, sometimes without punctuation or even a space. The first two digits stand for the hour, and the last two digits show the number of minutes after the hour.

To change from the 24 hour clock to the 12 hour clock, subtract 12 from the first two digits if they are greater than 12.

15:30 becomes 15:30 minus 12, which is 3:30 p.m.

Ed has just arrived to catch the 16:20 train. This is the time by his watch.

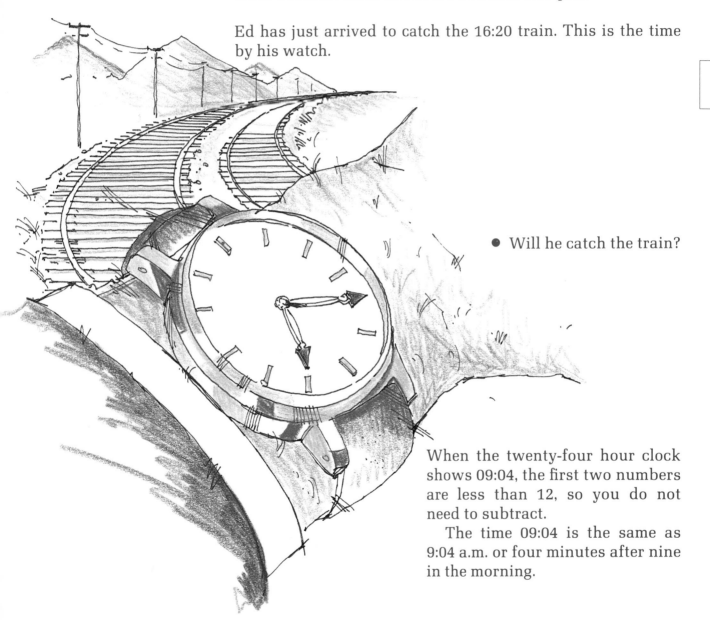

● Will he catch the train?

When the twenty-four hour clock shows 09:04, the first two numbers are less than 12, so you do not need to subtract.

The time 09:04 is the same as 9:04 a.m. or four minutes after nine in the morning.

Clock This

● Match each 24 hour clock time to the same 12 hour clock time.

Time Check

Check your knowledge of time facts with this puzzle. There is a question in each square and four possible answers.

● Select the correct answer and write down the letter at the end of the arrow.

● Write down the letter each time. Answer the question that the correct letters spell out.

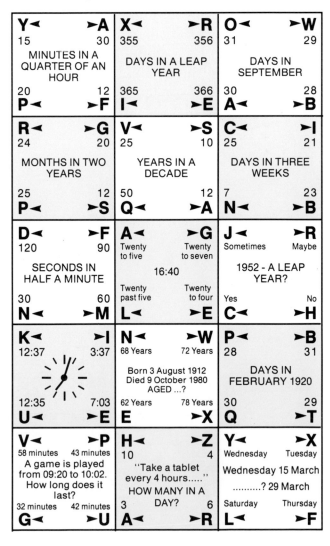

Y◄ 15 ►A 30 MINUTES IN A QUARTER OF AN HOUR 20 P◄ 12 ►F	X◄ 355 ►R 356 DAYS IN A LEAP YEAR 365 I◄ 366 ►E	O◄ 31 ►W 29 DAYS IN SEPTEMBER 30 A◄ 28 ►B
R◄ 24 ►G 20 MONTHS IN TWO YEARS 25 P◄ 12 ►S	V◄ 25 ►S 10 YEARS IN A DECADE 50 Q◄ 12 ►A	C◄ 25 ►I 21 DAYS IN THREE WEEKS 7 N◄ 23 ►B
D◄ 120 ►F 90 SECONDS IN HALF A MINUTE 30 N◄ 60 ►M	A◄ Twenty to five ►G Twenty to seven 16:40 Twenty past five L◄ Twenty to four ►E	J◄ Sometimes ►R Maybe 1952 - A LEAP YEAR? Yes C◄ No ►H
K◄ 12:37 ►I 3:37 12:35 U◄ 7:03 ►E	N◄ 68 Years ►W 72 Years Born 3 August 1912 Died 9 October 1980 AGED ...? 62 Years E ►X 78 Years	P◄ 28 ►B 31 DAYS IN FEBRUARY 1920 30 Q◄ 29 ►T
V◄ 58 minutes ►P 43 minutes A game is played from 09:20 to 10:02. How long does it last? 32 minutes G◄ 42 minutes ►U	H◄ 10 ►Z 4 "Take a tablet every 4 hours....." HOW MANY IN A DAY? 3 A◄ 6 ►R	Y◄ Wednesday ►X Tuesday Wednesday 15 March ....? 29 March Saturday L◄ Thursday ►F

Time Trap

28

The Coopers' home was burgled during the day while it was empty. The police have three suspects who all have alibis for part of the day. Sid, the sneak thief, was at the race track from 3:00 p.m. until 3:40 p.m. Vic, the vandal, had an appointment with his probation officer from 2:30 p.m. to 3:15 p.m. T. Leaf, the professional burglar, was meeting with his accountant from 2:15 p.m. until 4:00 p.m.

The police have taken statements from George and Melissa Cooper and their children, Cindy and Al, to try and establish when the burglary could have taken place. The times are expressed using the 24 hour clock.

● Which of the three suspects could have committed the crime?

George
"I left home for work at 0830. I came back at lunch time for some papers I had forgotten. I got home at 13:30, found the papers, had a cup of coffee and returned to work after 25 minutes. I got home from work again at 18:00 hours."

Melissa
I drove Al to school at 08:45 and returned after thirty minutes. I went shopping at 14:00 hours and then stopped by to see my sister. I was away two and a quarter hours. I came home and began preparing dinner.

Cindy
"My first class at college was at 10:00 hours, so I left home half an hour before. I came home at 13:30 and had an hour for lunch. I went to see a friend to get some notes for an essay. That took half an hour. Then I worked on my essay in my room until 17:30."

Al
Mom drove me to school and I arrived at 08:55. I got the bus home and arrived at 15:50.

Timetables

Look at this train timetable.

Maintown	d	11 30			12 05	12 50	13 05	13 30	13 50		14 05
Colburg	d	12 25	12 51	13 10	13 18	13 51	14 18	14 25	14 51	15 10	15 18
St Hilary's	d	12 35		13 21				14 35		15 21	
Highpoint	d	12 37		13 23				14 37		15 23	
Westford	d	12 41		13 27				14 41		15 27	
Ennerton	d	12 45		13 31				14 45		15 31	
Sumton	d	12 39		13 35				14 49		15 35	
Winderly	d	12 53		13 39				14 53		15 39	
Townside	a	12 58	13 08	13 43	13 34	14 06	14 34	14 56	15 06	15 43	15 34
Knowear	d		13 13	13 53	13 41	14 13	14 41		15 13	15 53	15 41
Fairhil	d		13 16	13 56	13 44	14 16	14 44		15 16	15 56	15 44
Wotchum	a		13 19	13 59	13 47	14 19	14 47		15 19	15 59	15 47
Crowsend	a	13 04	13 18		13 45	14 18	14 45	15 04	15 18		15 45
Maintown	d		17 00	17 30	17 50	18 03	18 50	19 30	19 50	20 30	20 50
Colburg	d	17 10	18 01	18 25	18 51	19 22	19 51	20 25	20 57	21 30	21 57
St Hilary's	d	17 21		18 35		19 35		20 35		21 40	
Highpoint	d	17 23		18 37		19 37		20 37		21 42	
Westford	d	17 27		18 41		19 41		20 41	21 03	21 46	22 03
Ennerton	d	17 31		18 45		19 45		20 45		21 50	22 07
Sumton	d	17 35		18 49		19 49		20 49		21 54	22 12
Winderly	d	17 39		18 53		19 53		20 53		21 58	
Townside	a	17 43	18 16	18 56	19 06	19 56	20 06	20 56	21 13	22 01	22 18
Knowear	d	17 53	18 23		19 13		20 13		21 20	22 09	22 28
Fairhil	d	17 56	18 26		19 16		20 16		21 23	21 12	22 31
Wotchum	a	17 59	18 29		19 19		20 19		21 26	22 15	22 34
Crowsend	a		18 23	19 04	19 18	20 04	20 18	21 04	21 25	22 09	22 30

- **1.** What do the gaps mean?
- **2.** What do *a* and *d* stand for?

● **3.** Which clock does it use?

● **4.** How long does the journey from Maintown to Crowsend take if you catch the 11:30 train?

● **5.** How long does the same journey take on the 20:30 train?

● **6.** If you live at Westford what is the latest train you can catch to be in Fairhill by 7:30 p.m.?

● **7.** Is the 12:05 an "express" train or a "local" train?

● **8.** Sue has to meet Theresa outside Ennerton library at 2:15 p.m. The library is a five minute walk from the station. Which train should she catch from Colburg?

Check your answers on page 62. If you scored 6 or more, you can turn to question 4 on page 33.

How Long Does it Take?

06:00 News
06:10 Local News
06:20 Weather
06:30 Financial Report
07:08 Cartoon Special
07:43 Breakfast Magazine
09:24 Farming Today
10:15 Making History
12:04 Lunch Box

● **1.** How long does the weather report last?

This is easy. It begins at 6:20 a.m. and ends at 6:30 a.m. It lasts 10 minutes.

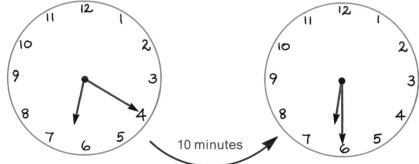

How long does the "Breakfast Magazine" run?

From 7:43 a.m. to 9:24 a.m. is more than an hour, so break the period up into stages.

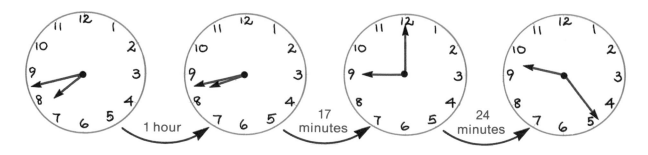

1 hour 41 minutes

● **1.** How long is it from the beginning of "Farming Today" to the start of "Lunch Box?"

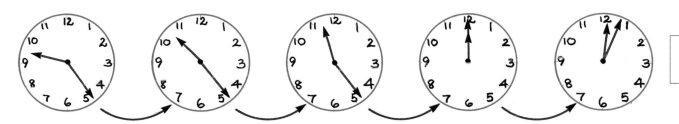

33

● **2.** If you turn on the TV to see the weather report, keep on watching the "Financial Report" and turn it off when "Cartoon Special" starts, how long will this take?

● **3.** How long is it from the start of "Breakfast Magazine" to the beginning of "Making History."

Work out the hours first and then the minutes.

● **4.** In the laboratory, there are two flasks which hold the same volume. There is one amoeba in one flask and two amoebas in the other. An amoeba can reproduce itself to form two amoebas in three minutes.

● It takes the two amoebas in the second flask three hours to fill it completely. How long does it take the amoeba in the other flask to fill it completely?

Answers to pages 32 and 33

1. It is 2 hours and 40 minutes from the beginning of "Farming Today" to the start of "Lunch Box."
(1 hour + 1 hour + 36 minutes + 4 minutes)

2. It takes 48 minutes.

3. From 07:43 to 09:43 is 2 hours. From 09:43 to 10:00 is 17 minutes. From 10:00 to 10:15 is 15 minutes.
The total time = 2 hours and 32 minutes.

4. It takes the single amoeba 3 minutes to reproduce itself. There are then two amoebas in the flask. It will take them 3 hours to fill the flask. The total time is 3 hours and 3 minutes.

34

Puzzle

● Find the sum of the numbers on a clock face **without** adding them all up.

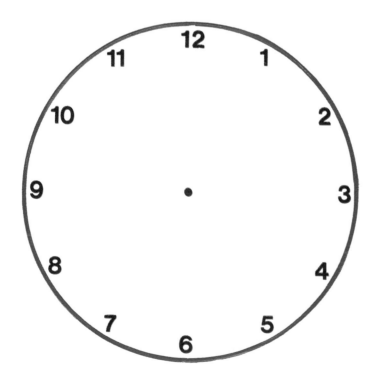

Investigation

● How long would it take you to count to a million?

Often it helps to break an investigation down into simple parts and build up to the answer.

1. Time yourself counting to 10. How many numbers did you say every second?

2. Time yourself counting to 100. How many numbers did you say every second?

3. How do you explain the difference between your answers to **1** and **2**?

4. As the numbers you are counting get bigger, will you count more or fewer of them each second?

5. Decide on a reasonable amount of numbers per second and calculate your answer.

Answer to page 34

This is one way of working out a reasonable estimate of how long it would take to count to a million.

1. It took 3 seconds to count from 1 to 10. This is $3\frac{1}{3}$ numbers per second.

2. It took 50 seconds to count from 1 to 100. This is 2 numbers per second.

3. Numbers like twenty-four take longer to say than single numbers.

4. Usually the bigger the number the longer it takes to say. For example, one hundred and fifty-five thousand three hundred and twenty-seven takes about 2 seconds to say.

5. An estimate of one number per 2 seconds is reasonable, although it would probably take a little longer. You have to stop for breath now and then! We are assuming you do not make any mistakes.

To calculate the total time it would take

2 million seconds $=$ (2,000,000 $\div$ 60) minutes $=$ 33,333 minutes (to the nearest minute)

33,333 minutes $=$ (33,333 $\div$ 60) hours $=$ 556 hours (to the nearest hour)

556 hours $=$ (556 $\div$ 24) days $=$ 23 days (to the nearest day)

It would take approximately 23 days to count to a million if you could do it without stopping. You would have to stop to eat and sleep. It would probably take you about 30 days all together.

Two ways of totaling the numbers on a clock face without adding them all up.

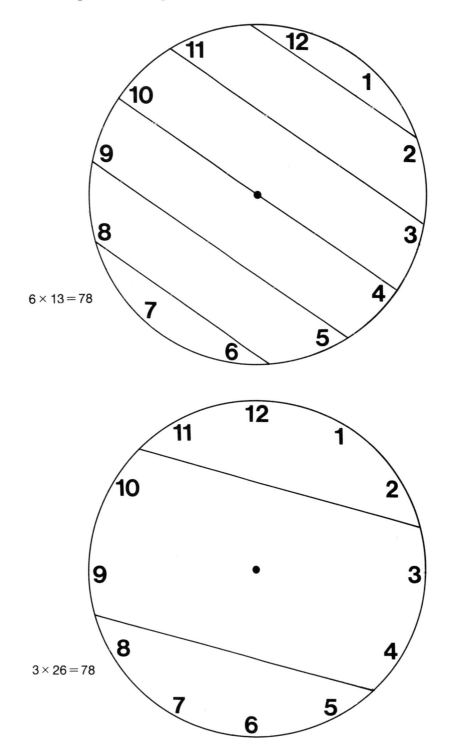

$6 \times 13 = 78$

$3 \times 26 = 78$

Calculating Distance

38

This diagram shows the distances between six towns. It is not a true map because it is not drawn to scale. It shows the approximate position of each town in relation to the others. The number shown between each pair of towns is the distance in miles between them.

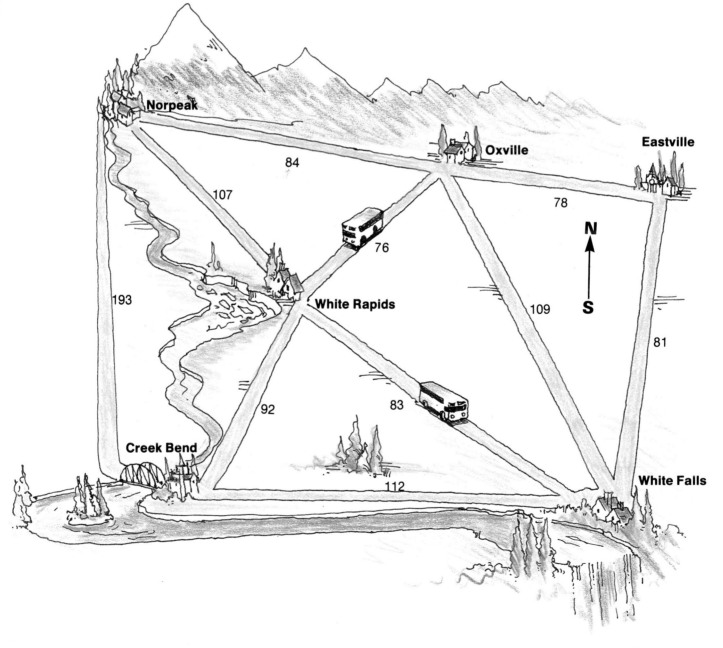

- **1.** What is the distance from Norpeak to Oxville?

- **2.** What is the distance from Norpeak to Eastville?

- **3.** How many possible routes are there from White Falls to Norpeak via White Rapids without traveling South?

- **4.** How many possible routes are there from White Falls to Norpeak via Oxville without traveling South?

- **5.** How else can you get from White Falls to Norpeak?

- **6.** Which is the shortest route from White Falls to Norpeak?

- **7.** How long is it?

- **8.** Landscape Tours is based at White Rapids. They run a two day circular coach trip from there to Creek Bend, White Falls, Eastville and Oxville. The cost of the trip includes a night's accommodation, breakfast and dinner.

- Landscape Tours must charge 40 cents per mile per person to make a profit. What is the fare for the trip to the nearest dollar?

Check your answers on page 43 before you continue with the next page.

Road Maps

This road map shows the main routes between various towns. The scale is shown underneath it .

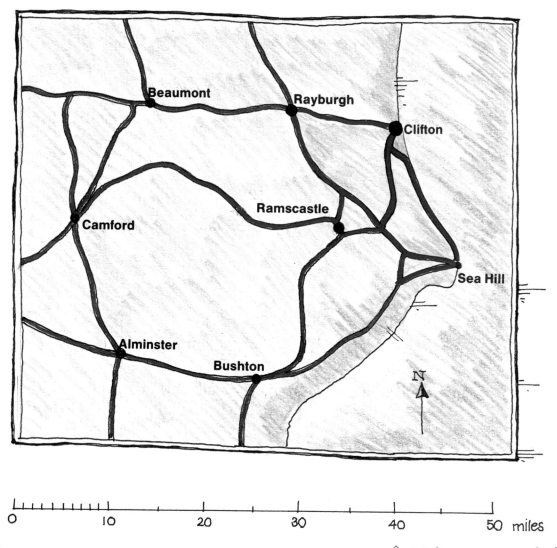

◇ Make a copy of the distance chart opposite. Notice that the towns are arranged in alphabetical order.

◇ You need a piece of thread or thin string. Place one end of the string on the map over the dot that marks Camford. Follow the turns in the road with the string and mark with your fingernail where Alminster is.

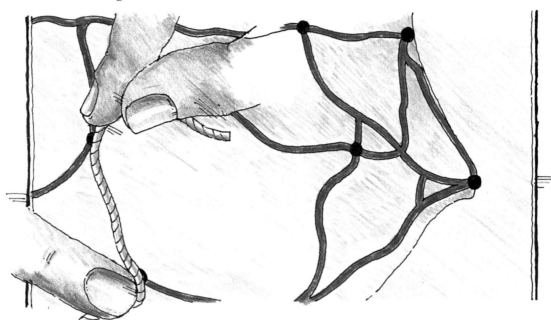

◇ Pick up the string. Straighten it out and lay it along the scale to work out how many miles it is between the two towns.

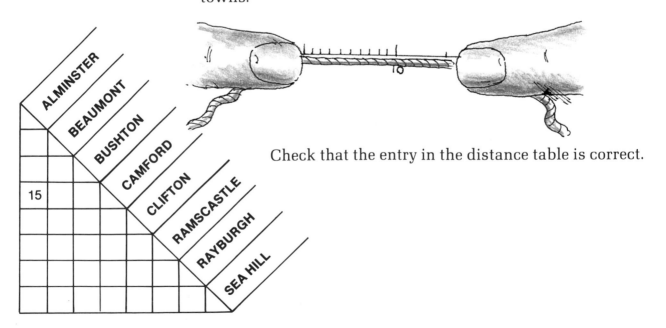

Check that the entry in the distance table is correct.

- In the same way, find the shortest distance between
a) Camford and Ramscastle
b) Ramscastle and Seahill

- Use the answers to **a** and **b** to fill in the distance from Camford to Seahill.

Your chart should now look something like this.

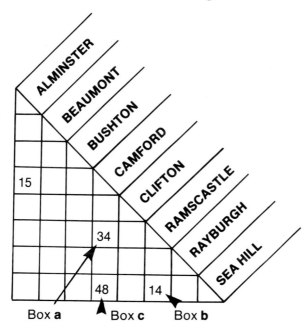

The mileage may be different by one or two miles, but the numbers should be in the same boxes. The number in box **c** must be the sum of the numbers in boxes **a** and **b**.

- What is the minimum number of measurements you must take in order to be able to complete the chart?

- Measure the distances you need and fill in their boxes on the chart.

Turn to page 44.

Answers to page 39

1. The distance from Norpeak to Oxville is 84 miles.

2. The distance from Norpeak to Eastville is $84 + 78 = 162$ miles.

3. There are four possible routes from White Falls to Norpeak via White Rapids without traveling south.
White Falls - White Rapids - Norpeak
White Falls - White Rapids - Oxville - Norpeak
White Falls - Creek Bend - White Rapids - Norpeak
White Falls - Creek Bend - White Rapids - Oxville - Norpeak

4. There are four routes from White Falls to Norpeak via Oxville without traveling south.
White Falls - White Rapids - Oxville - Norpeak
White Falls - Oxville - Norpeak
White Falls - Eastville - Oxville - Norpeak
White Falls - Creek Bend - White Rapids - Oxville - Norpeak

5. You can also go
a. White Falls - Creek Bend - Norpeak
b. White Falls - Eastville - Oxville - White Rapids - Creek Bend - Norpeak
c. White Falls - Oxville - White Rapids - Creek Bend - Norpeak
d. White Falls - White Rapids - Creek Bend - Norpeak

6. The shortest route is White Falls – White Rapids – Norpeak.

7. It is $83 + 107 = 190$ miles.

8. The round trip is $92 + 112 + 81 + 78 + 76 = 439$ miles. The cost to the nearest dollar would be $176.

Turn back to page 40.

43

You need a minimum of these twelve measurements. The numbers in the chart correspond to the route numbers on the map.

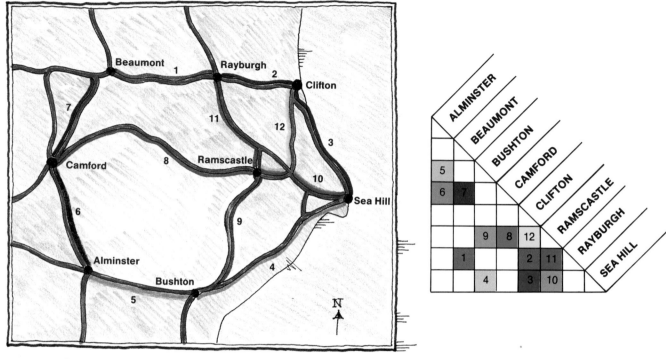

● Use these distances to calculate the rest of the distances needed to complete the chart. Where there is a choice of routes between two towns, calculate the shortest.

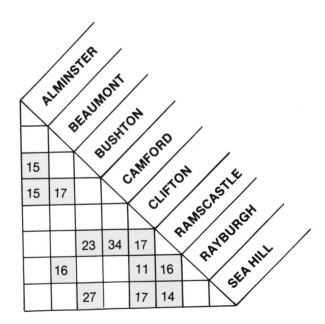

Balloon Speeds

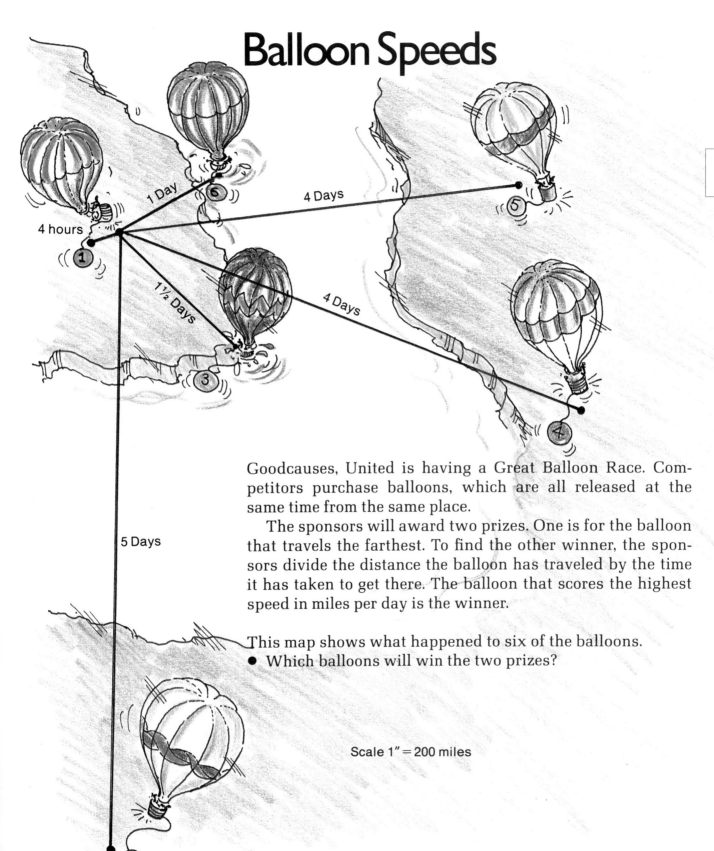

4 hours

1 Day

4 Days

1½ Days

4 Days

5 Days

Goodcauses, United is having a Great Balloon Race. Competitors purchase balloons, which are all released at the same time from the same place.

The sponsors will award two prizes. One is for the balloon that travels the farthest. To find the other winner, the sponsors divide the distance the balloon has traveled by the time it has taken to get there. The balloon that scores the highest speed in miles per day is the winner.

This map shows what happened to six of the balloons.
● Which balloons will win the two prizes?

Scale 1" = 200 miles

Balloon 2 will win the prize for traveling the greatest distance. It traveled 1,300 miles.

Balloon 1 traveled 50 miles in 4 hours = 300 miles per day (There are 24 hours in a day, so multiply by 6 to find how many miles the balloon would travel in a day at this speed.)

46

Balloon 2 traveled 1,300 miles in 5 days = 260 miles per day (Divide by 5 to find the distance for 1 day.)

Balloon 3 traveled 300 miles in $1\frac{1}{2}$ days = 200 miles per day (Divide by 3 to find distance for half a day, and then double for 1 day.)

Balloon 4 traveled 1,000 miles in 4 days = 250 miles per day

Balloon 5 traveled 800 miles in 4 days = 200 miles per day

Balloon 6 traveled 200 miles in 1 day

Balloon 1 will win the prize for the greatest speed in miles per day.

Constant Speed

When the balloons floated across the sky, they traveled faster or slower according to the wind. They did not travel at a constant speed. We do not often travel at a constant speed either.

Think about your journey to school. If you travel by car or bus, you will have to stop at stop signs and traffic lights. You will have to obey speed limits and vary your speed according to the amount of traffic around you.

If you walk, you will have to stop and look before crossing the street. Some sidewalks may be more crowded than others. You may walk slower uphill than down.

A machine can work at a constant speed. This machine can stamp out 100 cookies per second. It can stamp out 100 cookies every second until it is turned off or breaks down. It does not get tired or have a spurt of energy.

Average Speed

Concorde makes the journey from New York to London in approximately three hours. This is a distance of about 3,500 miles.

Concorde can cruise at 1,500 miles per hour (mph) but it does not travel at this speed for the whole trip. Its average speed is the distance it covers divided by the time it takes.

Concorde travels 3,500 miles in 3 hours.

Its average speed for the journey is
3,500 miles ÷ 3 hours = 1,167 mph
(to the nearest whole number).
The average speed is less than 1,500 mph because it must go slower at take off and landing.

The TGV, a special passenger train, runs between Paris and Lyons. It makes the 264 mile journey in 2 hours.

● What is its average speed?

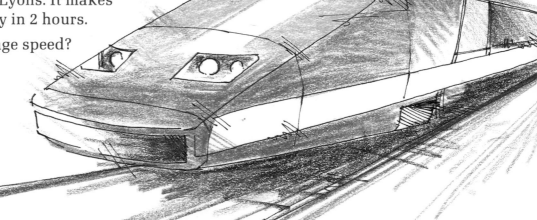

Units of Speed

A peregrine falcon making a **stoop** on its prey can reach a speed of 110 mph.

The sloth, the slowest moving land mammal, travels at 7 feet per minute.

Glaciers move between 1 and 24 inches per day.

The speed at which sound travels is related to the temperature of the air through which it travels. Sound travels faster near sea level than it does high in the atmosphere because temperature drops as you go higher.

At sea level sound travels through air at 1116 feet per second.

The speed of light is 186,420 miles per second.

Each speed measurement has two parts: a measurement of distance and a measurement of time.

SPEED = DISTANCE ÷ TIME

● **1.** Which travels faster through air, sound or light?

● **2.** What are suitable units of speed to measure the speed of a cheetah sprinting after its prey and the growth of a tree?

Knots

50

In the days of sailing ships, a knotted rope was let out over the side of a ship. The sailor, who was holding it, counted the number of knots which passed through his hands while sand ran through a timer. The number of knots was the speed of the ship.

Ships' speeds are still measured in knots. A knot is about 1.14 miles per hour.

A modern Atlantic liner travels at about 30 knots.

The Beaufort Scale

It was a sailor, Admiral Beaufort, who in 1805, invented a scale to estimate wind speed. Originally it was for use at sea but it has been adapted for land use. Admiral Beaufort observed the behavior of the waves and ships at different times and related them to different wind speeds. Later the Forces of the Beaufort Scale were matched to various wind speeds.

The Beaufort Scale ranges from Force 0 to Force 12.

Force 0 is calm; the wind speed is 0 to 1 mph; smoke rises vertically.

Force 6 is a strong breeze; the wind speed is 25 - 31 mph; large branches sway and umbrellas turn inside out. This is about as fast as a champion sprinter can run.

Force 12 is a hurricane; the wind speed is over 74 mph; a wind this violent causes widespread devastation.

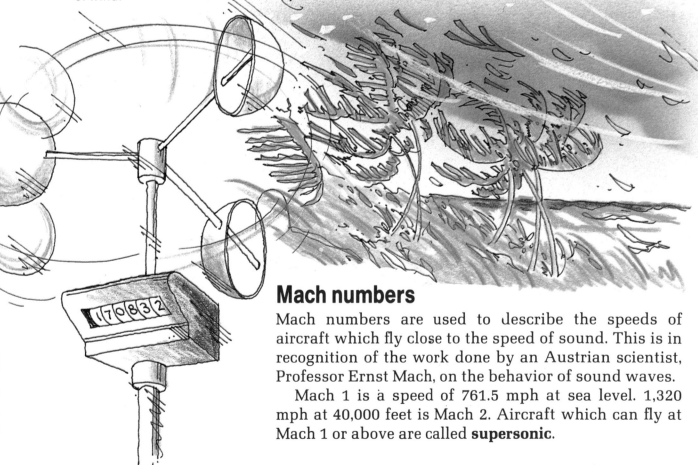

An anemometer is used to measure the force of wind.

Mach numbers

Mach numbers are used to describe the speeds of aircraft which fly close to the speed of sound. This is in recognition of the work done by an Austrian scientist, Professor Ernst Mach, on the behavior of sound waves.

Mach 1 is a speed of 761.5 mph at sea level. 1,320 mph at 40,000 feet is Mach 2. Aircraft which can fly at Mach 1 or above are called **supersonic**.

Answers to page 50

1. Light travels faster than sound.

2. A cheetah's speed is usually given in miles per hour. A tree's growth rate is measured in feet per year.

52 | Auto Racing

The first successful petrol-driven car was the Motor-wagen built by Karl Fredrich Benz in 1885. It had a top speed of 10 mph.

Today's racing cars can reach speeds of over 220 mph.

The Sportsville Grand Prix is run over this 3 mile circuit. It is a race of 80 laps.

● **1.** The race was won in 1991 by Vitorio Carina in a Heskerati in a time of 2 hours. What was his average speed?

● **2.** The fastest lap time was set up by James Sheppard in a Brabalpha in a time of 1 minute 10 seconds. What was his average speed?

● **3.** If the Motorwagen was driven at top speed for a lap, what would its lap time be?

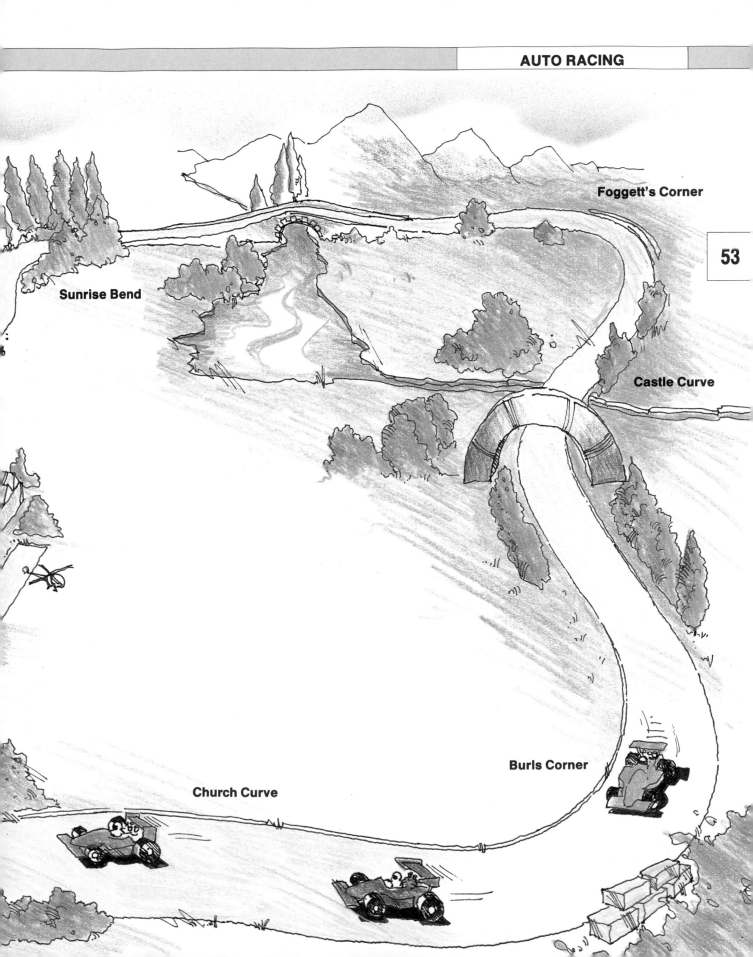

Travel Graphs

Journeys can be represented on travel graphs.

Use the **horizontal** axis for the time and the **vertical** axis for the distance.

Make sure that the scale on each axis is the same all the way along.

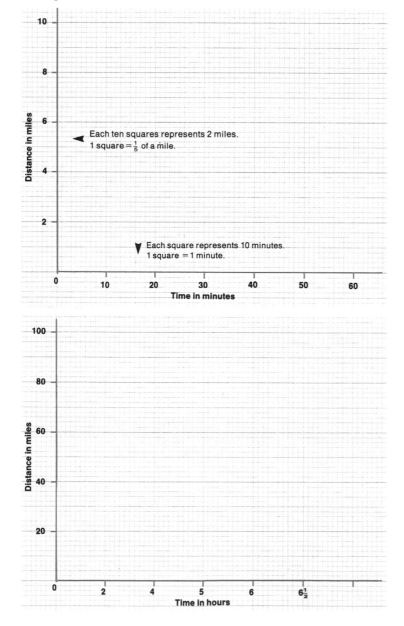

Each ten squares represents 2 miles.
1 square = $\frac{1}{5}$ of a mile.

Each square represents 10 minutes.
1 square = 1 minute.

● What is wrong here?

This graph represents a car journey of 130 miles which the Barnes family made to spend the day at the shore. It took them $3\frac{1}{2}$ hours.

Their average speed is represented by the red line on the graph. This is a straight line drawn from the start of the journey to its finishing time and distance ($3\frac{1}{2}$ hours – 130 miles).

We can find the average speed in mph by reading off the number of miles traveled in one hour. This is shown by the dotted line on the graph. The average speed from the graph is 36 mph.

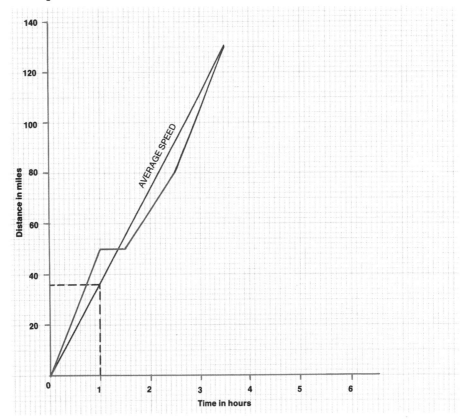

We can check this result by calculation.
130 miles in $3\frac{1}{2}$ hours $= 130 \div 3.5 = 37$ mph
(to the nearest whole number)

The difference between the results is due to the difficulty of being absolutely accurate when drawing lines on a graph.

The blue line shows the different stages of the journey.

The graph on page 55 can help you to work out the answers to these questions.

The Barnes left home at 8:30 a.m. and traveled through open countryside for one hour.

- **1.** How far did they travel in the first hour? What was their average speed?

They stopped to pick up a Sam, a friend of Jake's. Sam's Mom made them a cup of coffee and they had a chat.

- **2.** What was their average speed between 9:30 a.m. and 10 a.m.?

- **3.** What time did they leave Sam's house?

- **4.** From 10 a.m. until 11 a.m. they were driving through towns. What was their average speed for this part of the journey?

- **5.** From 11 a.m. they were driving along the highway to the coast. What was their average speed for the final part of the journey?

- **6.** What time did they arrive at the coast?

Answers to page 54

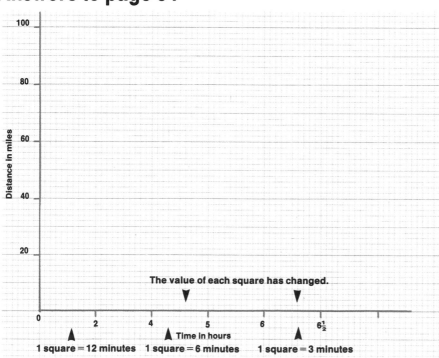

56

Draw a travel graph to represent this journey.

Juanita and Richard decide to travel from Mirani to Rogala, a distance of approximately 345 miles. They leave on the 08:30 train from Mirani station to travel to Bolene, a distance of 140 miles. The train travels at an average speed of 70 mph.

● **1.** What time do Juanita and Richard arrive at Bolene?

They have a drink and freshen up at the station. This takes half an hour.

● **2.** How do you show this on the graph?

Then they start to walk along Route 750 towards Rogala. They have covered 5 miles in an hour when a friend driving by offers them a lift. Fill in this part of the journey on the graph.

They complete the journey at an average speed of 50 mph.

● **3.** How far do they travel by car?

● **4.** What time do they arrive in Rogala?

A Tricky Problem!

● An express train leaves Chicago at the same time as a freight train leaves New York. The express train travels at an average speed of 80 mph and the freight train travels at an average speed of 50 mph. Which is the nearest to New York when they meet?

Assume that Chicago to New York is 780 miles.

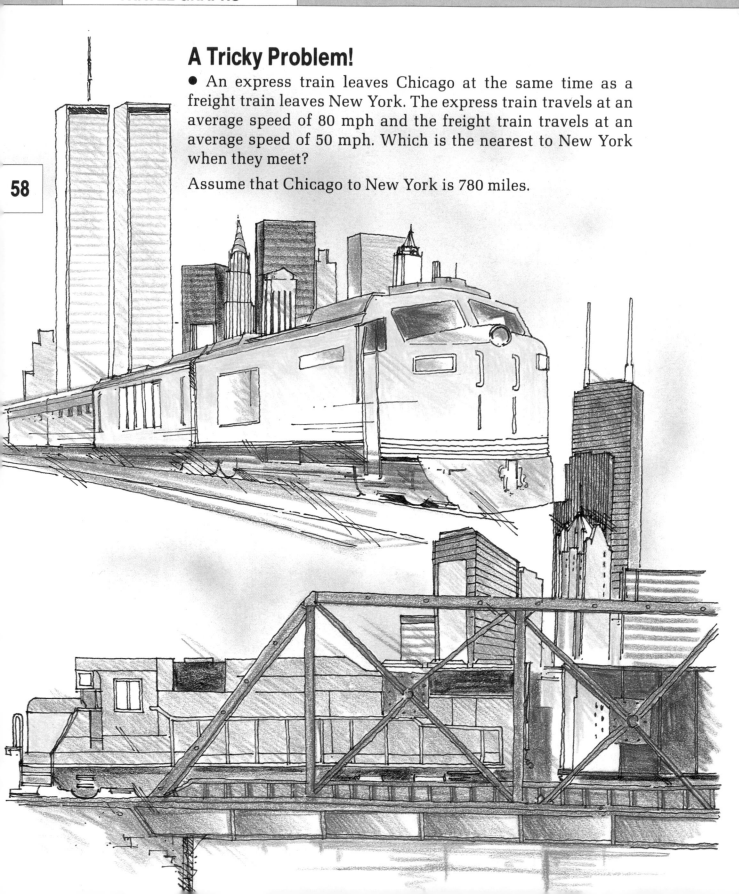

Number Square

7	9	6	4	0	2	6	5	8	3
	0	1	4	4	0	4	6	4	2
	1	8	5	1	9	5	2	0	2
9	7	0	7	0	1	7	4	1	4
	0	5	3	2	0	9	1	5	6
	2	3	1	6	3	1	2	3	8
	4	7	3	4	6	3	0	5	0
	1	6	0	7	8	5	0	7	2
	6	0	4	8	0	0	6	9	4
6	9	0	1	8	4	7	8	1	6

Copy the number square. Put a line through the answers to the clues, horizontally, vertically or diagonally. None of the answers are written backwards. Do not write on the book.

Clues

1. The number of days in a leap year.

2. The number of years in a decade and a half.

3. The number of months in a century.

4. The number of minutes in a day.

5. The number of seconds in a week.

6. The 11:10 train from Boston to New York arrives at 13:59. How nany minutes does the journey take?

7. Ebenezer Jones died on May 20, 1875 at the age of 69 years. His birthday was on June 17th. What year was he born?

8. Diana Edwards was born on September 5, 1926. How many months old was she on January 5, 1932?

9. A truck travels 624 miles in 12 hours. What is its average speed?

10. A car travels 300 miles at an average speed of 50 mph. The driver takes a lunch break of 50 minutes. How many minutes does the journey take?

Glossary

average speed the distance traveled divided by the time taken

axis the axis of the Earth is an imaginary line through from the North to the South Pole. The Earth rotates around its axis once everyday

calendar month a year is divided into twelve calendar months of different lengths

century one hundred years

decade ten years

horizontal a line drawn from side to side; it looks as if it is parallel with the horizon

lunar month the time the moon takes to orbit the Earth; a period of approximately 29 days

obelisk a tall column, usually made from one block of stone, with straight sides which taper to a pyramid at the top

orbit the path one heavenly body follows as it goes around another

stoop the steep dive a bird of prey makes to catch its victim

supersonic faster than the speed of sound

vertical a line drawn from top to bottom; a line at right angles to a horizontal line

Answers

Page 7
It takes the frog 36 hours. In 35 hours he climbs 35 feet. It takes him another hour to climb the last 5 feet.
It still takes five minutes to play the dance.
Page 9
1532 was the next leap year after 1531.
Page 10
1. 2150 will not be a leap year.
2. The first two figures tell you how many thousands and hundreds. 4 always divides exactly into any number of hundreds and thousands.
3. Selina is 12 years old.
4. Yes, 1200 was a leap year.
Page 11 There are approximately 348 days in 12 lunar months.
Page 12
The Earth is turning on its axis.
1. Shadows are shortest when the sun is at its highest at about 12 noon.
2. Sundials only work when the sun is shining.
Page 13
1. Different shapes and sizes of candles will burn at different rates.
2. Drafts will affect the rate at which the candle burns. Also they can be dangerous if they blow the flame onto something that will burn.
Page 16
See page 18

Page 17
See page 22
Page 19
This is the correct route and Justin Time.

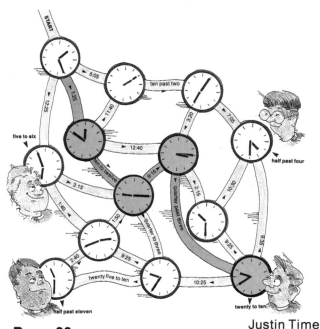

Justin Time

Page 20
See page 23
Page 21
See page 22
Page 25
Ed is two hours late.
Page 26
4 and a
6 and b
5 and c
1 and d
3 and e
2 and f
Page 27
100 (years in a century)
Pages 28 and 29
The only time the house was empty was between 2:30 p.m. and 3:00 p.m. Sid the sneak thief could have committed the crime.

Pages 30 and 31
1. The gaps mean the train does not stop at these stations.
2. *a* and *d* mean "arrives" and "departs."
3. 24 hour clock
4. 1 hour and 34 minutes
5. 1 hour and 39 minutes
6. 17:27
7. an "express" train
8. 13:10
Pages 32 and 33
See page 34
Page 34
See page 37
Page 35
See pages 36-37
Page 39
See page 43
Page 44
Your completed distance chart should look like this if you used the given measurements.

ALMINSTER	BEAUMONT	BUSHTON	CAMFORD	CLIFTON	RAMSCASTLE	RAYBURGH	SEA HILL
32							
15	47						
15	17	30					
55	27	40	44				
38	32	23	34	17			
48	16	39	33	11	16		
42	44	27	48	17	14	28	

Page 45
See page 46
Page 48
The average speed of the TGV is
264 miles ÷ 2 hours = 132 mph

Page 50
See page 52

Page 52
1. 240 miles in 2 hours = 120 mph average speed

2. 3 miles in 70 seconds
$= 3 \times 60$ miles in 70 minutes
$= 3 \times 60 \times 60$ miles in 70 hours
$= 3 \times 60 \times 60 \div 70$ miles in 1 hour
$= 154$ mph

3. At 10 mph it takes 6 minutes to travel 1 mile. To travel 3 miles takes 18 minutes.

Page 54
See page 56

Page 56
1. The Barnes family traveled 50 miles in the first hour at a speed of 50 mph.

2. Their average speed between 9:30 a.m. and 10 a.m. was 0 mph.

3. They left Sam's house at 10 a.m.

4. Their average speed through the towns was 30 mph.

5. On the final part of the journey they traveled 50 miles in an hour; their average speed was 50 mph.

6. The journey took $3\frac{1}{2}$ hours; they arrived at the shore at 12 noon.

Page 58
1. Juanita and Richard arrive at Bolene at 10:30 a.m.

2. Show the stop with a horizontal line; time is passing but no distance is traveled.

3. They travel 200 miles by car.

4. They arrive in Rogala at 4:00 p.m.

Page 58
When they meet, the two trains are in the same place. They are both the same distance from New York.

Page 59
Answers to the clues

1. 366 days

2. 15 years

3. 1,200 months

4. $60 \times 24 = 1,440$ minutes

5. $60 \times 60 \times 24 \times 7 = 604,800$ seconds

6. 169 minutes

7. 1805

8. 64 months

9. 52 mph

10. 410 minutes

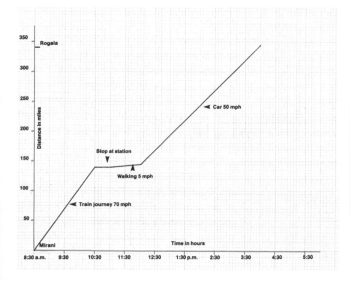

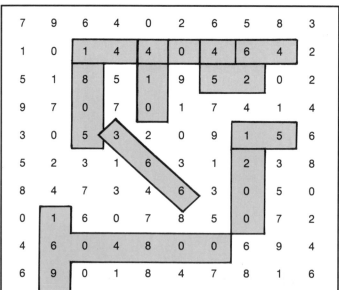

Index

64